Cover illustration: A pilot and his more casually dressed gunner pose with their late-model SB2C. This 'Beast' wears the overall glossy Sea Blue colour scheme adopted in October 1944. Note the Chromate Green turret and liferaft housing in the rear cockpit, the yellow liferaft itself and the red innersurfaces showing through the perforations of the flap. (USN/NARS via Stan Piet)

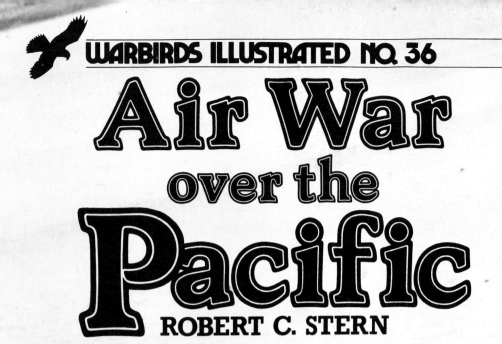

WARBIRDS ILLUSTRATED NO. 36

Air War over the Pacific

ROBERT C. STERN

ARMS AND ARMOUR PRESS

Introduction

Published in 1986 by Arms & Armour Press Ltd.,
2–6 Hampstead High Street, London NW3 1QQ.

Distributed in the United States by Sterling
Publishing Co. Inc., 2 Park Avenue, New York,
N.Y.10016.

British Library Cataloguing in Publication Data:
Stern, Robert C.
Air war over the Pacific.—(Warbirds illustrated;
v. 36)
1. World War, 1939-1945—Aerial operations
2. World War, 1939-1945—Pacific Ocean
I. Title   II. Series
940.54′26   D785.U63

ISBN 0-85368-735-8

Editing, design and artwork by Roger Chesneau.
Typesetting by Typesetters (Birmingham) Ltd.
Printed and bound in Italy
by GEA/GEP in association with
Keats European Ltd., London.

◀2
1. (Title spread) A small coastal steamer is straddled
by bombs dropped by a pair of SB2C Helldivers from
Randolph (CV-15), 14 July 1945, Hokkaido. During a
series of carrier raids that lasted from 1 July to mid-
August, anything that moved on water in the seas
around Japan drew the attention of marauding carrier
aircraft, and very little remained afloat by the war's
end. (USN/NARS)
2. The launch officer is about to give the 'go' to this
TBF-1 on the port catapult, *Independence* (CVL-22),
mid-1943. This was a period of working-up for new
ships and air groups prior to the beginning of the
Central Pacific offensive in October 1943. (NASM)

As suggested by the title of this work, the photo essay that follows is
intended to depict the appearance and activities of US naval aircraft
during the Second World War. This should by no means be taken as
an attempt to describe the entirety of the Allied air war against Japan:
that effort can readily be divided into four widely separated theatres of
operation, and three of these – China–Burma–India, the South-West
Pacific and the Aleutians – were almost exclusively land-based
campaigns employing very few naval aircraft and so receive very little
attention in these pages. It is on the remaining theatre that this book
concentrates.

The Central Pacific campaign of the US Pacific Fleet can be roughly
divided into three phases (reflected in the organization of this book):
early raids and battles in the South and Central Pacific from Pearl
Harbor to Midway (December 1941–June 1942); the battle for the
Solomons and Rabaul (August 1942–August 1945); and the 'island-
hopping' campaign across the Central Pacific (October 1943–August
1945). Not surprisingly, photographic coverage of the first phase and
the early parts of the second is somewhat sparse, but once the tide of
the war turned more resources were lavished on recording the details
of life on board the aircraft carriers and around the island airstrips
from which naval aircraft flew. The result was a happy abundance of
excellent photography of the Wildcats and Corsairs, the 'Beasts' and
the 'Turkeys' that are the subject of this book.

A note on aircraft camouflage colours is probably in order. The
colour photos reproduced in this book are reasonably accurate in their
portrayal of US Navy aircraft camouflage but, given the effects of
forty years on original Second World War-vintage colour material,
some verbal description of the colours might also be useful. The basic
US Navy camouflage colours were Insignia White, Light Gray, Sea
Gray (sometimes called Blue Gray), Intermediate Blue and Sea Blue,
all except Insignia White being shades of grey with varying amounts
of blue mixed in. Unlike the ship camouflage colours with similar
names used at the time, these paints had no red tint: Light Gray was a
pale pure cool grey; Sea Gray was a medium blue-grey; Intermediate
Blue was nearly identical in value to Sea Gray but was slightly bluer;
and Sea Blue was a dark blue-grey. All of these shades were available
in gloss or non-specular (matt) finishes, with the glossy versions often
looking like very different colours.

Some description of the organization of naval aircraft units might
help an understanding of the story. The basic unit was the squadron,
designated by the letter 'V' and followed by one or more mission
codes and a squadron number; hence VF-20 was the 20th Fighter
Squadron. Other common mission codes were 'B', 'S', 'T', 'P' and
'C', standing for Bomber, Scout, Torpedo, Patrol and Composite
missions respectively. An 'M' in the sequence indicated a Marine
Squadron, VMSB-211, for example, being a Marine scout bomber
squadron. Squadrons were organized into Carrier Air Groups (CVGs)
for duty on aircraft carriers, and it was common for an air group's
squadrons to be raised simultaneously and share the group's sequence
number. The composition of a CVG varied considerably throughout
the war, but a typical later war unit was CVG-9 on *Yorktown* in March
1945 which comprised VF-9, VB-9, VBF-9 and VT-9. Land-based
Marine squadrons were organized into Marine Air Wings (MAWs).

I would like to thank a number of people and organizations without
whose help these photographs could never have been collected. These
include Mike Hatfield of Vought Aircraft, Harry Gann of Douglas
Aircraft and the patient staffs at the US National Archives and the
Defense Audiovisual Agency. In particular, I would like to express
profound gratitude to Dana Bell of the Smithsonian Institution and
Stan Piet who assisted in tracking down the ever-elusive
contemporary colour photographs.

Robert C. Stern

▲3 ▼4

3. This flight of TBD-1 Devastators of VT-6 from *Enterprise* (CV-6) in 1939 shows the almost gaudy markings carried by prewar US Navy aircraft: the base paint was aluminium, but very little of that showed through by the time all the additional colours were painted on. Wing upper-surfaces were Chrome Yellow; tail and stabilizers were painted in the carrier identification colour, true blue for *Enterprise*; '6-T-16', being sixth section leader, carried fuselage and full cowl bands as well as wing chevron in Lemon Yellow; and tail markings, including the landing assistance stripe, were white. All other lettering was black, as were the wing walks. (USN/NHC)

4. On 30 December 1940 a basic camouflage scheme of overall non-specular Light Gray was ordered for all carrier aircraft. National insignia were to be displayed in four places – both sides of the fuselage, on the port wing uppersurface and on the starboard wing underside – and lettering was to be white. This is the scheme carried by this deckload of Wildcats, Dauntlesses and Devastators of CVG-3 aboard *Saratoga* (CV-3), mid-1941. (NASM)

5, 6, 7. In October 1941 the basic camouflage scheme was modified to require that all surfaces visible from above be painted non-specular Sea Gray, the line where the colours met to be wavy and blended. Immediately after Pearl Harbor, aircraft lettering was changed from white to black, whilst to aid quick identification of American aircraft thirteen alternating red and white stripes were to be painted on the rudder and the national insignia were to appear in six positions, greatly increased in size. The primary unit assigned the defence of Pearl Harbor in the very early days of the war was VMF-2, stationed at MCAS Ewa. Brewster F2A-3 Buffaloes of VMF-2 are here seen in camouflaged revetments at Ewa in February 1942.(USN/NARS)

5▲

6▲   7▼

▲8 ▼9

8. Shortly thereafter, VMF-2 was redesignated VMF-221 and sent to Midway Island, where it was decimated in June 1942. One of VMF-221's Buffaloes is seen being loaded on board *Kitty Hawk* (APV-1) at Pearl Harbor, March 1942, for transport to Midway. (USN)

9, 10. A PBY-5 of VP-11 being hoisted aboard *Tangier* (AV-8), 8 March 1942. The markings on this Catalina are absolutely standard for the time (note the wing roundels to both port and starboard). The exact location for these photographs is not known but *Tangier*

operated from Midway atoll during this period. (USN/NARS)

11. An early SBD is pushed on to an outrigger for stowage on board *Enterprise* (CV-6), 17 April 1942. The outrigger was a trough for an aircraft's tailwheel that allowed it to be parked topside without taking up precious deck space. Note the practice bomb dispensers at the wing hardpoints. At this time *Enterprise* was escorting *Hornet* (CV-8), which was carrying Doolittle's raiders on the approach to Japan. (USN/NARS)

▲12   ▼13

12. As soon as *Enterprise* and *Hornet* could return to port and refuel, they left Pearl Harbor for the South Pacific. This view over *Enterprise*'s aft flight deck, with SBD-3s of VS-6 parked, shows *Hornet* at the end of a line of oilers and destroyers, 3 May 1942. Official pressure to make aircraft markings less informative to the enemy has led to the deletion of the squadron number from the fuselage markings. (USN/NARS)

13. *Enterprise* and *Hornet* arrived in the South Pacific too late to help at Coral Sea, but they were able to fill in for the two carriers knocked out at that battle. Here, deck crewmen on *Enterprise* do maintenance work on one of the crash barriers; behind, the tail of a Wildcat is visible. By this time, 20 May 1942, the two carriers were hurrying back to Pearl Harbor to meet the Japanese threat to Midway. (USN/NARS)

14. Markings changes 'in the field' were often made only as time permitted, and in the days leading up to the Battle of Midway time was a scarce commodity on board US Navy aircraft carriers. Since the order required the new roundel to be large, the latter had to be moved forward so as to fit, leaving some of the old insignia showing on this Wildcat. (USN/NARS)

15. 'F5', an F4F-3 on board *Enterprise* (CV-6) in the South Pacific, 15 May 1942, is an example of just such a hastily re-marked aircraft. Owing to loud complaints from pilots that they were frequently the mistaken targets of trigger-happy American gunners who shot at anything red, the order went out in May to remove the red centre from the national insignia and to modify the rudder stripes. These aircraft of CVG-6 have not only lost their red paint but even lack their white landing assistance stripes on the tail. (USN/NARS)

▲16

16. The first unit to equip with the new Grumman TBF-1 Avenger was VT-8 of *Hornet*'s CVG-8, seen here on 26 March 1942. Essentially this unit constituted a 'shadow' squadron working up the new aircraft while the 'real' VT-8, mounted on TBDs, was flying from *Hornet* (CV-8). (USN/NARS)

17. The Avengers of VT-8 arrived at Pearl Harbor too late to catch *Hornet* (CV-8), which had left for Midway, and six were detached and sent to Eastern Island, Midway, for use as land-based bombers. All attacked the Japanese fleet early on 4 June 1942, but, without fighter escort, five were shot down. The sole survivor, '8-T-1', seen here after the battle on 6 June 1942, was badly shot up with the radio operator dead and bombardier wounded, barely making it back to Midway. (USN/NHC)

18, 19. After the victory at Midway, American carriers returned to the South Pacific in late July 1942 in preparation for the Guadalcanal landings. *Enterprise* (CV-6) stopped at Tonga while Marines practised landing boat drill, and native sailors inspected their western counterparts. In these photographs, SBD-3s of VS-5 (previously from *Yorktown*, CV-5, sunk at Midway) show the markings of that squadron, the individual aircraft number on the fuselage and wing leading edge, and the mission code 'S' on the tail. (USN/NARS)

▼17

18▲ 19▼

14

20, 21. The invasion of Guadalcanal on 7 August 1942 marked the beginning of a vicious struggle for the mastery of the South Pacific, and the few remaining US Navy aircraft carriers were fully committed to the campaign, regularly striking at Japanese land positions when not engaging their enemy counterparts. *Saratoga* (CV-3) just missed the Battle of Midway, but was now heavily engaged, participating in the Battle of the Eastern Solomons, 24 August 1942. Here a TBF-1 of VT-8, its tailhook apparently not extended, snags the first barrier and comes to a halt down on *Saratoga*'s deck. (USN/NARS)

22. The final carrier battle of the early war period was the Battle of Santa Cruz, 26 October 1942. Both sides pitched their remaining carriers at each other – *Shokaku*, *Zuikaku* and two Japanese light carriers against *Hornet* (CV-8) and *Enterprise* (CV-6). A TBF-1C of VT-10 is seen preparing to launch from *Enterprise* soon after 0830hrs. Signboards give the course and speed of the target, a 'Jap CV', and tell the pilot to 'proceed without *Hornet*', whose air group is not ready to launch. By the end of the day, both sides were incapable of further offensive action, *Hornet* having been sunk and most of the remaining carriers damaged; it would be a year before either side felt strong enough to send carriers again into contested waters. (USN/NARS)

23. The immediate impetus for the invasion of Guadalcanal was the near-completion of an airfield on that island, threatening the sea lanes to Australia. As soon as the airfield, dubbed 'Henderson Field' by the new owners, was secure, aircraft from *Saratoga* (CV-3) and *Wasp* (CV-7) began making regular visits. This SBD-3 is probably from 'Sara's VB-3 or VS-3, at Henderson Field in September 1942. (USMC)

24. The Marines put land-based Wildcat and Dauntless units into Guadalcanal in August 1942. The action was fast and furious for the 'Cactus Air Force' (Guadalcanal was code-named 'Cactus'), with daily bombing and strafing runs and almost nightly bombardment by Japanese ships. The conditions were primitive at first, as is evident in this view of Marine SBD-3s, possibly of VMSB-232, waiting for the next mission, September 1942. (USMC)

22▲

23▲　　24▼

▲25

▲26 ▼27

25. USAAF P–400s from Australia briefly joined the fight for Guadalcanal. These sharkmouthed Airacobras of the 67th FS, 347th FG, flew out of Henderson Field during October 1942. They did not last long, but then neither did any other fighter unit involved in the 'meatgrinder' at Guadalcanal. Tours of duty were often measured in weeks. (USMC)

26. Six squadrons of Marine Wildcats were butchered on Guadalcanal before the island was secured. This F4F-3A of VMF-112 or VMF-122 is seen on Henderson Field in February 1943. After the fall of Guadalcanal in that same month, Henderson Field, no longer a simple grass strip, became the base for raids on Japanese facilities further up the Solomons chain. (USMC)

27. The primary offensive weapon of the 'Cactus Air Force' was the Grumman Avenger. The Marine crew of this TBF-1 confer with their crew chief prior to a mission, February 1943. The Avenger's engine is already running, ready for final check-out and take-off. (USMC)

28. A nostalgic look at the colourful liveries carried by prewar USN aircraft. One of the last aircraft to be painted in the prewar scheme was the prototype Curtiss Helldiver, XSB2C-1 (BuNo 1758), seen over upstate New York on her first flight, 18 December 1940. The scheme is overall aluminium paint with Chrome Yellow wing uppersurfaces. The wingwalk is black, as are (for unknown reasons) both sides of the horizontal tail and the undersides of the wing flaps. All the colours are glossy. (NASM)

29. A well-worn SBD-1 assigned to a scouting squadron, late 1942. The camouflage is the two-tone scheme, Sea Gray over Light Gray, authorized in October 1941. (Douglas Aircraft)

30. A three-tone SBD-5 being serviced at sea. The landing gear and the inside of the door are Chromate Green. The standard paint scheme for propellers was black with yellow tips. (USN/NARS via Stan Piet)

31, 32, 33. A new generation of Marine fighters arrived at Henderson Field on 11 February 1943 in the form of the F4U-1 Corsairs of VMF-124. Traditionally, the Marines only got the Navy's left-overs, but here they found themselves with the hottest fighter around, conservative Admirals considering the Corsair too tricky for carrier operations and approving it for land-based operations only. In this case, the Navy's loss was the Marines' gain as VMFs gleefully retired their old Wildcats for the new F4Us. These views show VMF-124 Corsairs on Guadalcanal in February 1943, on the flight line, being bore-sighted and warming up prior to a mission. (USMC)

◀30

31▲

32▲   33▼

34, 35, 36. Changes in camouflage and markings came rapidly in mid-1943. A new camouflage scheme, authorized on 1 February, called for a three-colour pattern with non-specular Sea Blue on the wing uppersurfaces, on the upper part of the fuselage and on any undersurfaces of folding wings that could be seen from above when the wing was folded, non-specular Intermediate Blue on the fuselage sides and the vertical tail, and non-specular Insignia White on the remaining undersides; the national insignia reverted to a four-position display. This new scheme was effective and popular, its only serious flaw being that it was difficult to apply and maintain. The change to the national insignia, on the other hand, was simple but very unpopular. Beginning on 29 June, the star and circle were to feature a white bar on each side, with a narrow red border around the entire design, but this new pattern lasted officially for less than three months. Gunners still fired at anything red, and the complaints of pilots soon led to the red surround giving way to blue. These SBD-5s on board *Cabot* (CVL-28) date from September 1943. (USN/NARS)

▲34

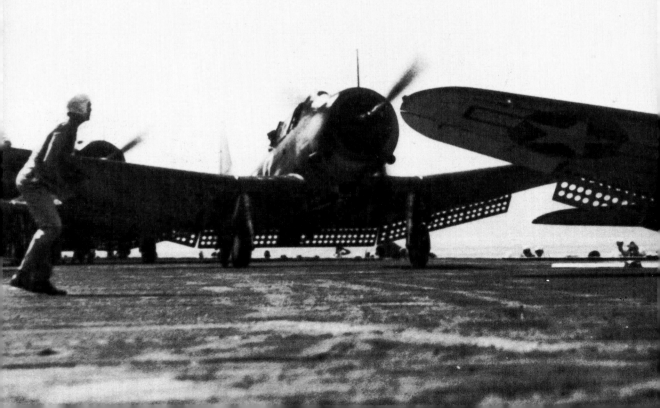

▲37

37. 'Daisy Mae' carries eight mission markers (yellow bomb insignia) on her fuselage, 9 July 1943; she is a TBF-1 on another ground support mission against Munda, a Japanese airbase on New Georgia Island established as a forward base for attacks on Guadalcanal. New Georgia was invaded on 30 June, but Munda did not fall until the end of the month. (USMC)

38. The Marines disliked the changes in camouflage and markings that were promulgated in mid-1943, and they resisted repainting their aircraft, with the result that the two-tone scheme could be seen in the Solomons well into 1944. Most Marine units refused to add the red surround to the national insignia, although they frequently added the bars. These F4U-1s are seen on Munda in September 1943. Both aircraft show the two-tone scheme and different non-standard or anachronistic insignia styles. (USMC)

39. A truck hauling 1,000lb bombs passes in front of a Marine TBF-1C on Munda, 28 October 1943. The airfield fell into Allied hands in August and was immediately used against its former owners. Again note the two-tone camouflage. (USN/NARS)

▲40 ▼41

40. The next step up the Solomons was Vella Lavella, bypassing the strongly held Kolombangara. An airfield was established at Barakoma Point by October and was soon a thriving fighter base. Here, plane captains wait on the runway while pilots are strapped into the F4U-1s, 1 November 1943. When the command was issued in September to paint out the red surround with blue, most Marine units complied, though unedged insignia could be seen throughout the remainder of the war. (USMC)

41. The name most associated with Marine Corsairs is that of Major Gregory 'Pappy' Boyington the almost legendary commander of the 'Black Sheep', VMF-214. While many of the stories surrounding Boyington are pure fiction, a few are true. One relates to the time that VMF-214 was running low on baseball caps, a Marine pilot's favourite non-flying headgear. Unable to requisition the standard-issue khaki kind, Boyington sent a letter to the then champion St.

Louis Cardinals offering to trade aerial victories for Cardinal caps. A deal was struck, ending in this 4 December 1943 swap on Vella, in which Boyington (right) gave up a fistful of victory insignia for a dozen caps. The aircraft is an F4U-1A, BuNo 17740. (USMC)

42. Another well-used fighter strip was established on the Russell Islands between Guadalcanal and Munda, VMF-123 operating from there in late 1943. Note the variety of styles of national insignia to be seen, 6 December. (USMC)

43. The final stop in the Solomons chain was the large island of Bougainville. Marines landed at Cape Torokina on 1 November 1943 and immediately began work on a series of airstrips, the first aircraft to land on the Torokina fighter strip being these SBD-5s of VB-98, 1 December 1943. VB-98 was one of a number of Navy squadrons that fought from land bases throughout the Solomons campaign. (USMC)

▲44

44. Another Navy squadron, VC-40, joined VB-98 at Torokina and the two units commenced daily raids on Rabaul and Kavieng in an attempt to neutralize those major Japanese bases in the Bismarck Archipelago. SBD-5s of both squadrons are seen here on 10 December 1943, one from VB-98 on the runway and one from VC-40 to the right. (USMC)

45. Three SBD-5s of VC-40 en route to Kavieng pass by Mount Bagana, an active volcano on Bougainville north-east of Cape Torokina, early 1944. These Dauntlesses carry the regulation three-colour camouflage scheme. (USN).

46. Even before the end of fighting on Bougainville, a further move was made towards Rabaul with the capture of the Green Islands midway between Bougainville and New Ireland. Navy Seabees, seen watching a Marine F4U-1A land, quickly established an airfield intended primarily as an emergency landing strip for aircraft damaged in the continuing raids on Rabaul but also serving as a base for a squadron of Marine Corsairs and RNZAF Tomahawks (background), 7 March 1944. (USMC)

47. There was no standard aircraft numbering scheme for Marine aircraft; each squadron found a system that suited its purposes. The Marine Corsair unit on the Green Islands strip among others used the last three digits of the Bureau Number, a unique identification number assigned to each individual aircraft acquired for the Navy and Marines by the Navy's Bureau of Aeronautics – hence the apparently random numbers seen on these F4U-1As and on those in the last view. A unit could have both a '941' and a '941A' because BuAer would sometimes, for book-keeping reasons, allocate to an aircraft a number already given to another, but with a letter suffix. (USMC)

▼45

▲48 ▼49

50▲

48. The Central Pacific campaign swung into high gear with the invasion of Tarawa Atoll in the Gilberts in November 1943. On the 25th of that month, the airstrip on Betio Island became the home base for the F6F-3s of VF-1, which had been flying air support missions from *Barnes* (CVE-20) and *Nassau* (CVE-16). Unlike their counterparts in the Solomons, almost all the air units involved in the Central Pacific campaign carried up-to-date camouflage and markings, witness these three-tone Hellcats. (USMC)

49, 50. SBD-5s of VB-10 from *Enterprise* (CV-6) circle their carrier after returning from action in March 1944. CVG-10 participated in raids on widely separated targets during this month, hitting Emirau in the Bismarcks on the 22nd and the Palaus on the 29th. Note the simplicity of the markings on the Dauntlesses, a condition that would soon come to an end as the number of carriers in action increased and the need arose to distinguish one air group from another. (NASM)

51. A pair of rocket-armed TBM-1Cs of VT-15 from *Essex* (CV-9), 10 May 1944. These aircraft also carry the recently adopted narrow white tailband of *Essex*'s air group, just prior to that carrier's first action, the Marcus raid on 19–20 May. (USN/NARS)

51▼

▲52　▼53

52, 53, 54. The operations of an aircraft carrier would have been impossible were it not for the services of hundreds of deck crewmen who guided the big machines through their 'ballet' on deck. These views show SB2Cs of VB-15 being guided to a landing and parked aboard *Essex* (CV-9) during operations in April and May 1944. A good LSO (Landing Signals Officer) was crucial to the smooth operation of an aircraft carrier: he controlled the approach of incoming aircraft through arm signals with his 'paddles', arms extended straight, as here, indicating a 'Roger Pass' or good approach. Once on board, the 'Beast' was immediately taxied forward under the control of a deck officer to clear the landing area aft and finally parked forward with wings folded. Note the white tail stripe in the last of these views, 10 May 1944. This is an early example of the air group markings developed informally as the carrier groups grew. (USN/NARS)

55. The defenders on Marcus took their toll of the attackers. This SB2C-1C of VB-15 lost part of its rudder to ground fire over Marcus on 20 May 1944 but made it safely back to *Essex*. (USN/NARS)

55▼

▲56

56. A bad landing would sometimes tear up the flight deck surface of a carrier like *Essex* (CV-9), seen here during the Marcus raid of 20 May 1944. US carriers, until the launching of the late-war Midway Class, all had unarmoured wooden-surfaced flight decks, and carpenter's mates were always on duty to repair or replace planks. (USN/NARS)

57. Another carrier whose air group adopted distinctive markings early in 1944 was *Hornet* (CV-12). Here an SB2C-1C of VB-2 has just ditched, a not uncommon fate for 'Beasts' when they were first

introduced, 21 February 1944. The group marking is the white dot just under the tail number. (USN/NARS)

58. A torpedo for an Avenger is hauled aft past an SB2C-1C of VB-2 (foreground), an F6F-3 of VF-2 (left) and an F6F-3N of VFN-76, June 1944. The carrier is *Hornet*. (USN/NARS)

59. A portrait of a 'Turkey', a TBM-1C of VT-2 operating from *Hornet* (CV-12), June 1944. This aircraft also carries the white dot on its tail, and an unusual feature is the squadron insignia just forward of the cockpit. (NASM)

▼57

▲60

60, 61. Unable to build Hellcats fast enough and unwilling to assign Corsairs to carrier duty, the US Navy had to find a fighter to stock the fighter section of the VCs (composite squadrons of fighters and torpedo bombers) of its expanding fleet of escort carriers. The answer was a virtual copy of the Wildcat, the Eastern FM-2. The new Wildcat could be distinguished from its predecessor by the large indented exhaust trough just behind the cowling and above the wing leading edge. These FM-2s were among the first to see service, flying off *Windham Bay* (CVE-92), 10 June 1944. (USN/NARS)

62. Aircraft used for carrier training were often retired combat machines, such as this SBD-5. Little effort was made to keep up with changes in markings regulations, hence the red surround seen here late in the war. One consistent element in the markings of such aircraft was the use of large Insignia Yellow alphanumerical codes on wing and fuselage. (USN/NARS via Stan Piet)

63. Basic trainers, such as this N3N-1, were painted in overall Chrome Yellow. (USN/NARS via Stan Piet)

▼61

64. A TBM-1C takes off into an overcast sky from *Yorktown* (CV-10), 1944; the cruiser *New Orleans* (CA-32) is in the background. The Avenger is finished in standard midwar three-tone camouflage, looking very grey here because of the cloudy sky. (USN/NARS via Stan Piet)

65. An ex-USAF B-24J, serial number 42-64102, in partial Navy colours, China, 1945. What remains of the tail markings shows that this Liberator was formerly assigned to the 7th Bomber Group, 10th Air Force. The colours appear to be overall Sea Gray with abundant white polka dots on the undersides. Other markings include 'a bit of cheesecake' at the nose and red cowl bands. (NASM via Dana Bell)

66. The markings of escort carrier air units at this stage of the war generally included an alphabetic code to identify individual aircraft and sometimes a distinctive white pattern on the tail to identify the carrier. An FM-2 marked 'G6' is here being spotted on the catapult prior to launching off *Windham Bay* (CVE-92), 10 June 1944. Note the white tail-tip. (USN/NARS)

67. 'G8' at the moment of launch, *Windham Bay*, 10 June 1944. The catapult bridle, used to attach the main landing gear to the catapult, is dropping between the Wildcat's main wheels. Launch was always made with the canopy open, to aid rapid exit in case aircraft and pilot ended up 'in the drink'. (USN/NARS)

▲64 ▼65

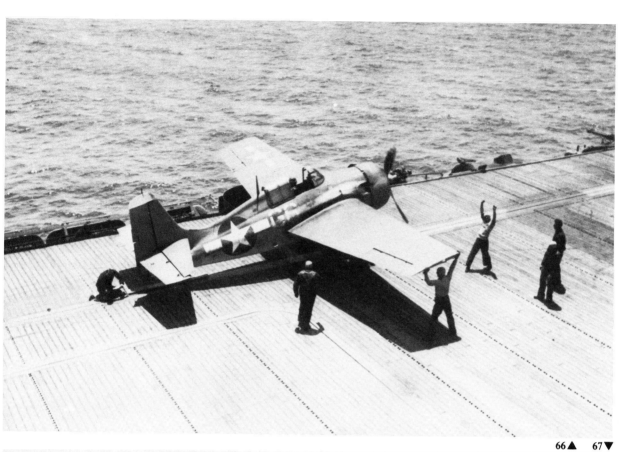

▲68 ▼69

68. The long-awaited invasion of the Marianas, Operation 'Forager', was immediately opposed by approximately 170 Japanese aircraft dispersed among seven airfields on Saipan, Tinian and Guam. The immediate targets of the defenders were the escort carriers providing close air support for the landings on Saipan. Here an 'Irving' (J1N1) dives in flames on *Coral Sea* (CVE-57), as seen from *Kitkun Bay* (CVE-71), 18 June 1944. Two TBM-1C Avengers of VC-5 can be seen on CVE-71's flight deck; note the alpha-numerical codes carried on the aircraft's tails. (USN/NARS)
69. The same attack seen from the target, *Coral Sea*. The Irving twin-engined fighter burns fiercely as it tries to hit the carrier. It missed. (USN/NARS)
70. The intensity of shipboard defence made life dangerous even for friendly forces. Here a Wildcat takes off from *Coral Sea* (CVE-57)

during a dusk attack on 17 June 1944 only to be greeted by 'friendly' anti-aircraft fire. (USN/NARS)
71. The first carrier confrontation since the Battle of Santa Cruz in October 1942 came when the Japanese reacted to the invasion of Saipan. On 19 June 1944, taking advantage of the longer range of his aircraft and anticipating the use of bases on Saipan, Tinian and Guam for refuelling and rearming, Admiral Ozawa sent wave after wave of aircraft off his nine carriers, a total of 324 aircraft. Hardly any of them found their target, the American carriers, but among the few to get close were nine 'Judys' that came in underneath the CAP (combat air patrol) shortly after 1400hrs. and attacked TG.58.2. This view over the aft flight deck of *Monterey* (CVL-26) towards *Wasp* (CV-18) shows the intense AA fire put up by those carriers, which escaped without damage. (USN/NARS)

▲72 ▼73

72. Swirling contrails in the sky were often all that could be seen of the action from the surface during the Battle of the Philippine Sea. At least 217 of the attackers were victims of aerial combat with Mitscher's Hellcats, and so complete and relatively easy was the victory that it became popularly known as 'The Great Marianas Turkey Shoot'. This photograph was taken from *Monterey* (CVL-26), 19 June 1944. (USN/NARS)

73. Spruance struck back the next day, and Mitscher's air groups went after Ozawa's now fleeing forces, catching them late in the day. Here the battleship *Haruna* and light carrier *Zuiho* manoeuvre in an attempt to avoid the attack of the Helldivers and Avengers. One carrier, *Hiyo*, was lost to the American attack, and two others, Pearl Harbor veteran *Shokaku* and the new *Taiho*, were lost to American submarines. However, this loss in carriers was not nearly so serious as the decimation of Ozawa's air groups: when Japanese carriers next sortied, they did so with flight decks virtually bare. (USN/NARS)

74, 75, 76. Newly captured airfields in the Central Pacific were home to Marine or Army Air Force fighter squadrons. These latter units, part of the 7th Air Force, often arrived at their assignments by somewhat unnatural means for USAAF aircraft – by aircraft carrier. The photograph shows P-47Ds of the 19th FS, 318th FG, launched off *Natoma Bay* (CVE-62) on 23 June 1944 and heading for Aslito Field on Saipan. Incredibly, none of the Thunderbolts was lost. The aircraft are finished in typical USAAF camouflage, olive drab over neutral grey; the lower cowling and tail are white, and the tailband is blue. (USN/NARS)

74 ▲

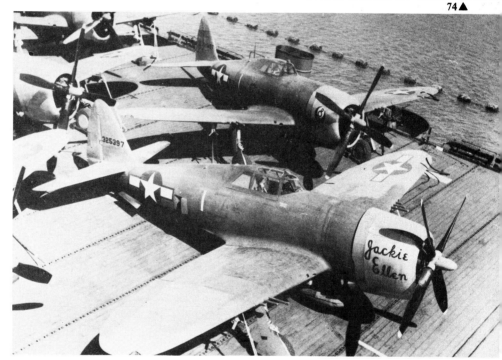

75 ▲ 76 ▼

KEEP CLEAR OF PROPELLERS

77–81. The efficiency of carrier deck crews in handling wrecks became legendary. With other aircraft in the group still airborne, possibly low on fuel or damaged and waiting for a clear deck, speed was of the essence. This sequence of five photographs shows the crash of SB2C-1C '18' of VB-2 on *Hornet* (CV-12), 3 July 1944. 'Beasts' suffered from 'hook bounce', meaning all too often that if the pilot failed to catch a wire at the moment his aircraft hit the deck, it was impossible to avoid the barrier. Barrier crashes frequently ended in an embarrassing and dangerous nose-dive into the deck, breaking the 'Beast's engine mounts, rupturing fuel lines and leading to a fire. Just such a sequence of events overtook '18'. Swarming deck crews put out the blaze with foam, pushed her over on to her landing gear and dragged her to the after lift for lowering to the hangar deck. Her eventual fate was probably to be pushed over the side. (USN/NARS)

79▲

80▲   81▼

82. Crash crews hurry towards a TBM-1C (BuNo 25162) of VT-31 after a barrier crash on *Cabot* (CVL-28), 11 July 1944. *Cabot*'s air group marking at this time was a white stripe down the trailing edge of the rudder. (USN/NARS)

▲ 83

84 ▲

◀ 85

83. Two months later, and another crash on *Cabot* (CVL-28): this time an F6F-5 (BuNo 58070) of VF-44 snags the barrier, 11 September 1944. The air group marking has changed position, now running down the centre of the tail. In March of that year the basic camouflage for fighters had been changed to overall gloss Sea Blue, while that for other aircraft remained as before except that colours were to be glossy instead of non-specular. The changeover was slow to take place – active carriers had more important things to do than repaint aircraft – and it often became apparent only when new, correctly painted replacement aircraft arrived on board. (USN/NARS)

84. The next major target in the Central Pacific was the Philippines, raids intended to isolate island garrisons and soften up the defences beginning in September 1944. Avengers of VT-44 off *Cabot* (CV-28), still carrying the three-tone scheme, are seen here during a raid on coastal shipping off Negros Island, 12 September 1944. (USN/NARS)

85. Another Hellcat unit to convert to overall gloss Sea Blue camouflage was VF-20 of CVG-20 on *Enterprise* (CV-6), seen here on 16 October 1944; as on *Cabot*, the Helldivers and Avengers in the background retain the three-tone scheme. The air group tail marking carried by 'Big E's squadrons was a white triangle with the individual aircraft number in black. (USN/NARS)

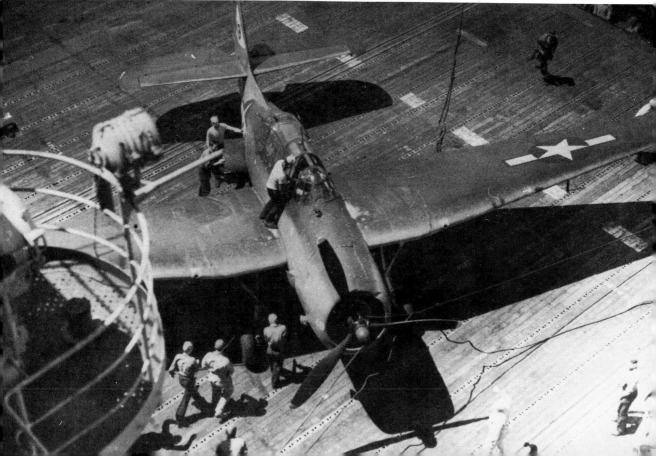

86, 87. Avengers on board *Enterprise* in late October 1944, during the action off Leyte and the Battle of Leyte Gulf. These TBM-1Cs of VT-20 were actively engaged in the Battle of the Sibuyan Sea, contributing to the sinking of the super-battleship *Musashi* on 24 October, and in the Battle off Cape Engano against Ozawa's remaining carriers on 25 October. (USN/NARS)

88. Some carriers continued to use simple numerical markings rather than distinctive air group designs: these SB2C-3s of VB-19 on *Lexington* (CV-16), 25 October 1944, carry large individual aircraft numbers on their tails. (USN/NARS)

89. Another example of extremely simple markings is this deckload of CVG-13 aircraft on board *Franklin* (CV-13), also on 25 October 1944. Deck crewmen are arming F6F-5 Hellcats with rockets and SB2C-3 Helldivers with bombs prior to the air group's participation in the Battle off Cape Engano. (USN/NARS)

88▲   89▼

▲90
90. 'Ripper', an F6F-5 of VF-7, *Hancock* (CV-19), 6 November 1944. The carrier's air group marking was a white horseshoe, and note also the white propeller hub. The national insignia on gloss Sea Blue aircraft was often much simplified, the Insignia Blue circle and surround being simply deleted to leave the white star and bar. (USN/NARS)

91. TBF-1C Avengers over Leyte Island, the Philippines, 6 November 1944. The aircraft in the foreground is from VT-7, *Hancock* (CV-19); those in the background belong to VT-18, *Intrepid* (CV-11), and carry the white cross tail insignia of that carrier. (USN/NARS)

▼91

92. An SB2C-4 of VB-7 from *Hancock* about to ditch, 4 November 1944. This 'Beast' has a narrow white cowl band, another marking carried by some of the aircraft of *Hancock*'s air group. The 'turtleback' aft of the gunner's position has been lowered to facilitate his exit from the aircraft after ditching. (USN/NARS)
93. Somebody has to foul up the system! Contrary to standard practice, whereby markings 'belonged' to the carrier and obliged an

air group to change markings when reassigned to another carrier, CVG-20 claimed the white triangle as its own and retained that marking when it transferred from *Enterprise* (CV-6) to *Lexington* (CV-16) at the end of 1944. In this photograph, a TBM-1C of VT-20 is seen over Cam Ranh Bay after raiding Japanese shipping there, 12 January 1945. (USN/NARS)

94. US naval aircraft flew not only from American decks: as the naval threat in Europe eased, the Royal Navy assigned carriers to the war in the Pacific, carriers whose air groups were largely composed of American aircraft. Typical was this Avenger II (TBM-1C) ready on the catapult on HMS *Illustrious*, 17 December 1944. (US Army)

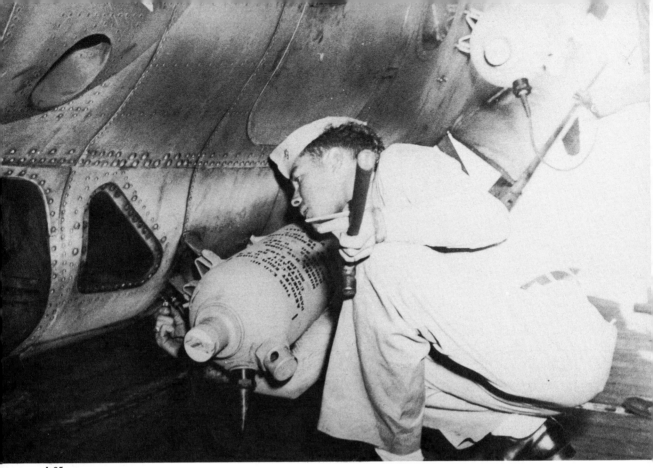

▲95

95, 96. One method of increasing the weight limits of aircraft operating off the short decks of escort carriers was JATO (Jet-Assisted Take-Off), involving the attachment of small aft-pointing rocket bottles which could be fired electrically by the pilot to provide additional boost at launch. An early JATO system was tested on a TBF-1 off *Shipley Bay* (CVE-85), 31 January 1945. This initial trial proved the feasibility of the system, which saw some limited use during the Pacific war and widespread use postwar. (USN/NARS)

▼96

97. An SB2C-4 of VB-20 banks low over the water returning to *Lexington*, 19 February 1945. (USN/NARS)

98. The great variety of informal markings, the confusion caused by air groups like CVG-20 retaining markings and the fact that some air groups never adopted distinctive insignia led COMAIRPAC on 27 January 1945 to issue the so-called 'G' markings, a set of standardized white geometrical designs for all fleet and light carrier air groups, a move reinforced on 7 February by Mitscher's order to expedite adoption of the new markings. As a result, the 'G' symbols rapidly appeared on most carrier aircraft early in 1945. This view

shows TBM-3s of CVG-84 on board *Bunker Hill* (CV-17) in February 1945. The 'G' symbol is the upward-pointing (forward-pointing on wings) white arrow. Note, however, that the underwing arrow is black for visibility against the white undersurfaces (this is a late example of the retention of three-tone camouflage – overall gross Sea Blue was ordered for all carrier aircraft on 7 October 1944!). For the initial carrier raids on Tokyo, which came on 16–17 and 25–26 February, many air groups carried a white or yellow cowl band as a temporary marking; the band on the Avenger is white. (USN/NARS)

▲99   ▼100

99, 100. Two more photographs showing CVG-84 aircraft bearing 'G' symbols: an SB2C-4E (illustration 99) and an F4U-1D. The Navy finally relented and cleared Corsairs for carrier duty; this example has a yellow cowl band. (USN/NARS)

101. Another air group to adopt the cowl band for the Tokyo raids was *Wasp*'s (CV-18). This F4U-1D of VBF-68 is seen on deck on 18 March 1945. The 'G' symbol, modified slightly from the original directive, was a broad horizontal white band on the tail, repeated on the starboard wingtip. (USN/NARS)

102, 103. Possibly the most spectacular of the 'G' symbols was the double-triangle pattern assigned to *Essex* (CV-9). The three-tone TBM-3 trying to find a hole in the wash over the bow carries this marking on tail and starboard wing, 22 February 1945. The other view shows crewmen looking over at the burning *Bunker Hill* (CV-17), the victim of a kamikaze off Okinawa, 11 May 1945. Lined up along the deck-edge are Corsairs, Helldivers and Avengers, all in the overall gloss Sea Blue scheme and all carrying the 'G' symbol. (USN/NARS)

104, 105. Crewmen from another carrier, *Randolph* (CV-15), also watch *Bunker Hill* burn, 11 May 1945. F6F-5s are seen on *Randolph* wearing that carrier's 'G' symbol scheme, three Sea Blue bands on an otherwise white vertical tail and on white ailerons. (USN/NARS)

104▲ 105▼

106, 107. Rockets for Corsairs. Armourers on board *Bennington* (CV-20) assemble 5in HVARs (High Velocity Artillery Rockets), 26 February 1945. Note the F4U-1Ds of VMF-112 or VMF-123 in the background carrying *Bennington*'s 'G' symbol, a white arrowhead, on ailerons and tail. (USN/NARS)

▲108 ▼109

108. The 5in HVAR was assembled from a rocket body, which was nothing more than a slightly modified 5in shell, and a rocket motor. Here, *Bennington*'s armourers attach the warheads. (USN/NARS)

109, 110. A pair of TBM-3s of VT-17 from *Hornet* (CV-12), seen over the rugged coast of Okinawa, 17 April 1945. VT-17 is obviously in transition from three-tone to the proper over-all gloss Sea Blue camouflage, but both aircraft carry the correct 'G' symbol markings, two white squares on the tail and both wingtips. (USN/NARS)

111. In assigning 'G' symbols, an attempt was sometimes made to provide consistency with previous markings. *Ticonderoga* (CV-14), which had previously carried a 'V' on its aircraft's tails as its distinctive marking, was now given an inverted triangle as its assigned 'G' symbol, as seen on this SB2C-4E of VB-87, 24 May 1945. (USN/NARS)

112. When CVG-9 replaced CVG-20 on board *Lexington* (CV-16) in late February 1945, the squadron brought with it the correct 'G' symbol for that carrier, a downward-slanting white band borne on tail and starboard wingtip. This SB2C-4, about to meet an inglorious end, carries the official markings, 7 June 1945. (USN/NARS)

110▲

111▲ 112▼

▲113 ▼114

113. Escort carrier air groups continued operations into 1945 without a markings system like the 'G' symbols, and many air groups, such as MCVG-4 (Marine Carrier Air Group 4) operating off *Cape Gloucester* (CVE-109), still used alphanumerical codes to distinguish the aircraft of different carriers. Here an F4U-1D of VMF-351 snags the barrier, 7 April 1945. (USN/NARS)
114, 115. The relative success of the 'G' symbols for the bigger carriers led to the adoption of a similar system for escort carriers in an order dated 2 June 1945. Because of the large number of escort carriers and because they were generally assigned to operating divisions of eight ships, the markings scheme allocated a white tail and wingtip marking to each division and distinguished between division members by means of differing numbers and of differing locations for narrow fuselage and wing stripes in white, yellow or light green. Excellent examples are seen in these views of aircraft of MCVG-4 from *Cape Gloucester* (CVE-109). The division marking

(of Carrier Division 27) was the white band mid-tail and mid-wing, and two vertical stripes (probably yellow, possibly light green, but definitely not white) are carried. The F4U-1D, 5 July 1945, has lost its port wingtip in a barrier crash; it retains its alphanumerical codes, which are painted the same colour as the stripes. The TBM-3s, en route to Shanghai on 29 July 1945, are similarly marked: they carry individual aircraft numbers on their tail (barely distinguishable here), again in the same colour as the stripes. (USN/NARS)
116. As if fighting the Japanese were not enough, nature sometimes proved to be as great an enemy. Three times during 1944–45 the Pacific Fleet sailed into typhoons it might have avoided, and paid a heavy price in lost ships and lives. The last of these came just before the Japanese surrender. This view is aft along the flight deck on board *Wasp* (CV-18), looking into a seemingly endless world of water, rain and spray, 26 August 1945. (USN/NARS)

▲117 ▼118

117, 118. Almost as serious as the loss in ships was the devastation caused by the typhoons in the carrier air groups. Understandably, smaller carriers suffered more than fleet carriers. The suffering Avenger (photograph 117) is a TBM-1C of VT-28 that was thrown around the hangar deck on board *Monterey* (CVL-26) during the first and possibly the worst of the typhoons, 19 December 1944. Photo 118 shows an SB2C-4 thrown up on the wing of an Avenger in the hangar on board *Windham Bay* (CVE-92) after the second typhoon, off Okinawa, 6 June 1945. (USN/NARS)

119. The 'G' symbols did indeed standardize markings, but several problems remained. Admiral McCain, in tactical command of Third

Fleet carriers, complained that the symbols were hard to remember and difficult to describe over the radio, and on 27 July 1945 he ordered the adoption of a system of one- or two-letter codes in their place. This F6F-5 of VF-86, *Wasp* (CV-18), has that carrier's code letter, 'X', on its tail and wingtip, 24 August 1945. (USN/NARS)

120. Under the new alphabetic code scheme, *Ticonderoga* (CV-14) got its 'V' insignia back again on tail and aileron, as seen on these SB2C-4s of VB-87, August 1945. Because of the lateness of the changeover, many air groups never adopted the new scheme and ended the war still carrying 'G' symbols. (USN/NARS)

120▼

▲121 ▼122

121, 122. Just too late for the war, a squadron of Grumman F7F-2N Tigercats, VMF(N)-533, sets out for the front on board *Windham Bay* (CVE-92), August 1945. The Tigercat was something of an orphan child: designed as a long-range fighter, fighter-bomber and night-fighter when carriers were scarce, it found each of its intended roles filled by existing carrier aircraft. Eventually the Navy did with its Tigercats what it did with any aircraft for which it had no use – it gave them to the Marines. (USN/NARS)